NOSTALGIA FOR THE ABSOLUTE

NOSTALGIA FOR THE ABSOLUTE

Massey Lectures, Fourteenth Series

by George Steiner

Canadian Broadcasting Corporation

ISBN 0-88794-076-5

Printed in Canada for
CBC PUBLICATIONS
BOX 500, STATION A, TORONTO M5W 1E6
by The Hunter Rose Company

The five radio broadcasts published here were given in the fall of 1974 as the fourteenth series of Massey Lectures. They were organized and produced by Paul Buckley of the *Ideas* unit of the CBC Radio Arts Department. Begun by the CBC in 1961 to enable distinguished authorities in fields of general interest and importance to present the results of original study or research, the lecture series was named in honour of the Rt. Hon. Vincent Massey, former Governor General of Canada.

GEORGE STEINER is a writer and scholar of international reputation whose work displays not only distinguished literary qualities, but wide inter-disciplinary scope, and an incisive interest in the study of language. He was born in Paris, France, and there received his first academic degree. Moving to the United States, he received his B.A. in 1948 from the University of Chicago. In 1950 he received his M.A. from Harvard University, where he was awarded the Bell Prize in American Literature. From 1950 to 1952 he was a Rhodes Scholar at Oxford University, England, and there received his Ph.D. He joined the staff of the *Economist*, London, and later was a member of the Institute for Advanced Studies, Princeton. In 1959 he was the recipient of the O.Henry Short Story prize. At the present time he is Professor of English and Comparative Literature, Université de Genève, Switzerland, and Extraordinary Fellow, Churchill College, Cambridge, England. He is also chief literary critic of *The New Yorker* magazine. Dr. Steiner is the author of *Tolstoy or Dostoevsky; The Death of Tragedy; Anno Domini; Language and Silence; In Bluebeard's Castle; Some Notes Towards the Re-definition of Culture; Extraterritorial: Papers on Literature and Language Revolution; Fields of Force;* and the forthcoming *After Babel*.

CONTENTS

The Secular Messiahs   1

Voyages into the Interior   12

The Lost Garden   24

The Little Green Men   38

Does the Truth Have a Future?   50

The conjecture which I want to put forward in these Massey Lectures is a very simple one.

Historians and sociologists agree, and after all we should sometimes believe them too, that there has been a marked decline in the role played by formal religious systems, by the churches, in Western society.

The origins and causes of this decline can be variously dated and argued, and, of course, they have been. Some would locate them in the rise of scientific rationalism during the Renaissance. Others would assign them to the scepticism, to the explicit secularism, of the Enlightenment with its ironies about superstition and all churches. Still others would maintain that it was Darwinism and modern technology during the industrial revolution which made systematic beliefs, systematic theology, and the ancient centrality of the churches so obsolete. But the phenomenon itself is agreed upon. Gradually, for these very complicated and diverse reasons, the Christian faiths (may I emphasize this plural) which had organized so much of the Western view of man's identity and of our function in the world, whose practices and symbolism had so deeply pervaded our daily lives from the end of the Roman and Hellenistic world onward, lost their hold over sensibility and over daily existence. To a greater or lesser degree, the religious core of the individual and of the community degenerated into social convention. They became a kind of courtesy, an occasional or perfunctory set of reflexes. For the very great majority of thinking men and women—even where church attendance continued—the life-springs of theology, of a transcendent and systematic doctrinal conviction, had dried up.

This desiccation, this drying-up, affecting as it did the very centre of Western moral and intellectual being, left an immense emptiness. Where there is a vacuum, new energies and surrogates arise. Unless I read the evidence wrongly, the political and philosophic history of the West during the past 150 years can be understood as a series of attempts—more or less conscious, more or less systematic, more or less violent—to fill the central emptiness left by the erosion of theology. This vacancy, this darkness in the middle, was one of "the death of God" (remember that Nietzsche's ironic, tragic tonality in using that famous phrase is so often misunderstood). But I think we could put it more accurately: the decay of a comprehensive Christian doctrine had left in disorder, or had left blank, essential perceptions of social justice, of the meaning of human history, of the relations between mind and body, of the place of knowledge in our moral conduct.

It is to these issues, on whose formulation and resolution society and individual life depend for coherence, that the great "anti-theologies", the "meta-religions" of the nineteenth and twentieth centuries, address themselves. These are very awkward terms and I apologize for them. "Meta-religion", "anti-theology", "surrogate creed"—they are awkward but also useful tags. Let me try and pull them together in these five talks by using a general term. I want to propose to you the word "mythology".

Now in order to qualify for the status of a mythology, in the sense in which I am going to try and define it, a social, a psychological, or a spiritual doctrine or body of thought must fulfil certain conditions. Let's have a look at these. The body of thought must make a claim of totality. That sounds very simple-minded, and in a way it is. Let me try and sharpen the idea. What do we mean by its being total? It must affirm that the analysis which it puts forward of the human condition—of our history, of the meaning of your life and mine, of our further expectations—is a total analysis. A mythology, in this sense, is a complete picture of "man in the world".

This criterion of totality has a very important consequence. It allows, it invites, if the mythology is an honest and serious one, disproof or falsification. A total system, a total explanation, falls down when and where a substantive exception, a really powerful counter-example, can be produced. It is no use trying to patch up a little corner here or adding a bit of glue or string there. The construct collapses unless it is a whole. If any of the central mysteries, sacramental mysteries, of Christianity or of the life of Christ or his message were to be totally disproved, it would be no good trying to do a quick repair job on one corner of the structure.

Secondly, a mythology in the sense in which I am using the word, will have certain very easily recognizable forms of beginning and development. There will have been a moment of crucial revelation or diagnostic insight from which the entire system springs. This moment and the history of the founding prophetic vision will be preserved in a series of canonic texts. Those of you who are interested in the Mormon movement will easily recognize my image: an angel appearing to the founder of the whole movement and handing to him the famous golden plates, or the Mosaic law. There will be an original group of disciples who are in immediate contact with the master, with the founder's genius. Soon some of these disciples will break away into heresy. They will produce rival mythologies or sub-mythologies. And now watch something very important. The orthodox in the great movement will hate such heretics, will pursue them with an enmity more violent than that which they vent on the unbeliever. It's not the unbeliever they're afraid of—it's the heretic from within their own movement.

The third criterion of a true mythology is the hardest to define, and I ask you to bear with me because I hope it will emerge by force of example in these five talks. A true mythology will develop its own language, its own characteristic idiom, its own set of emblematic images, flags, metaphors, dramatic scenarios. It will breed its own body of myths. It pictures the world in terms of certain cardinal gestures, rituals, and symbols. As we proceed, I hope this will become entirely clear.

Now consider these attributes: totality, by which I simply mean the claim to explain everything; canonic texts delivered by the founding genius; orthodoxy against heresy; crucial metaphors, gestures, and symbols. Surely the point I am making is already obvious to you. The major mythologies constructed in the West since the early nineteenth century are not only attempts to fill the emptiness left by the decay of Christian theology and Christian dogma. They are themselves a kind of *substitute theology*. They are systems of belief and argument which may be savagely anti-religious, which may postulate a world without God and may deny an afterlife, but whose structure, whose aspirations, whose claims on the believer, are profoundly religious in strategy and in effect. In other words, when we consider Marxism, when we look at the Freudian or Jungian diagnoses of consciousness, when we look at the account of man offered by what is called structural anthropology, when we examine all these from the point of view of mythology, we shall see them as total, as canonically organized, as symbolic images of the meaning of man and of reality. And when we think about them we will recognize in them not only negations of traditional religion (because each of them is saying to us, look, we don't need the old church any more—away with dogma, away with theology), but systems which at every decisive point show the marks of a theological past.

Allow me to underline this. It is really the centre of what I'm trying to say, and I hope it is quite clear. Those great movements, those great gestures of imagination, which have tried to replace religion in the West, and Christianity in particular, are very much like the churches, like the theology, they want to replace. And perhaps we would say that in any great struggle one begins to become like one's opponent.

This is only one way, of course, of thinking of the great philosophic, political, anthropological movements which now dominate so much of our personal climate. The convinced Marxist, the practising psychoanalyst, the structural anthropologist, will be outraged at the thought that his beliefs, that his analyses of the human situation, are mythologies and allegoric constructs directly derivative from the religious world-image which he has sought to replace. He will be furious at that idea. And his rage has its justification.

I have neither the wish nor the competence to offer technical observations, for example, on the Marxist theory of surplus value, on the Freudian account of the libido or the id, on the intricate logistics of kinship and linguistic structure in Lévi-Strauss's anthropology. All I hope to do is to draw your attention to certain powerful, recurrent features and gestures in all these "scientific" theories. I want to suggest to you that these features directly reflect the conditions left by the decline of religion and by a deep-seated nostalgia for the absolute. That nostalgia—so profound, I think, in most of us—was directly provoked by the decline of Western man and society, of the ancient and magnificent architecture of religious certitude. Like never

5

before, today at this point in the twentieth century, we hunger for myths, for total explanation: we are starving for guaranteed prophecy.

The mythological scenario in Marxism , which I am beginning with in this first talk, is not only expressly dramatic, but is also representative of the great current of thought and feeling in Europe which we call romanticism. Like other constructs of social utopia, of secular, messianic salvation, which follow on the French revolution, Marxism can be expressed in terms of historical epic. It tells of the progress of man from enslavement to the future realm of perfect justice. Like so much of romantic art, music, and literature, Marxism translates the theological doctrine of the fall of man, of original sin, and of ultimate redemption, into historical, social terms.

Marx himself suggests an identification of his own role with that of Prometheus. Isn't it interesting, and in a way unsurprising, that when Marx was a young man the last thing he was planning to do was to write a major critique of political economy? Rather, he was working on an epic poem about Prometheus. And you can guess how the later scenario works. Bearing the destructive, but also cleansing, fire of truth, i.e., the materialist-dialectical understanding of the economic and social force of history, Prometheus/Marx will lead enslaved humanity to the new dawn of freedom. Man was once innocent, he was free of exploitation. Through what dark error, through what sombre felony did he fall from this state of grace?

This is the first of our theoretic problems and it is one of extreme difficulty. In each of the great mythologies or substitute religions we are looking at together, the nature of the original sin remains obscure or problematic. How did slavery arise? What are the origins of the class system? Marx's answer remains peculiarly opaque. Perhaps I can explain why. Like almost every post-romantic, particularly German, he was obsessed with the magnificence of ancient

6

Greece. He regarded the ancient Greek culture as the crown of man—artistically, philosophically, poetically, even in some ways politically. He knew full well about slavery and about the primitive development of Greek economy. So how could he reconcile his belief in the economic conditions of human well-being with what he knew of ancient Greek history? The answer is that he was too honest to lie about it and he never reconciled them. With one breath he speaks of the total excellence and eternal supremacy of ancient Greece, and with the next breath he tells us that the whole of human history is a great march forward into freedom and progress. We know from Marx that it is only with feudalism, and with the evolution of feudalism into mercantilism, and later, capitalism, that his epic diagnosis becomes confident. But the early writings, the famous 1844 manuscripts, show how explicitly theological was his image of the lost condition of man's innocence. I want to quote here because unless one goes back to these profoundly moving pages it is difficult to believe that we are listening to Marx and not, for example, to Isaiah. He's describing what this kingdom of innocence, this garden of perfect justice was like: "Assume," says Marx, "assume man to be man and his relationship to the world to be a human one. Then you can exchange love for love. Then you can exchange trust only for trust." This is a fantastic vision of the proper state of human society. And let us bear it in mind when we come back to questions of eros, of love, and of exchange between men, in later talks in this series. Instead, says Marx, man carries about on his very mind and body the lasting emblem of his fallen state. And what is that emblem? It is the fact that man is exchanging money instead of love for love and trust for trust. I quote again: "Money is the alienated ability—or perhaps I should translate genius or capacity—of mankind." Money is the alienated "mankindedness" of man—a dreadful condemnation when we think of the earlier vision of true innocence.

Now this sense of a distant catastrophe, of a cosmic disgrace—and may I put a hyphen in the word, a dis-grace, a falling from grace—comes through to us with vivid terror in the Marxist vision, as it does in Coleridge, in the "Ancient Mariner", or in Wagner's "Ring". Press more closely for definition, for historic location. Ask where did this horrible thing happen? What did we do wrong? Why have we been thrown out of the Garden of Eden? I don't think you really get a good answer. No less than Rousseau, Blake, or Wordsworth, Marx adopts almost unconsciously the romantic axiom of a lost childhood of man. Turning to the wonders of the Greek poets whom he loved so much; turning, as we have seen, though perhaps unconsciously, to the language of the prophets, Marx speaks, and I quote again, of "the social childhood of mankind where mankind unfolds in complete beauty". And when we ask again, with mounting impatience: What is the fall of man? What sin did we commit? Marxism does not really reply.

But there can be no doubt about the visionary messianic character of what it says about the future. If it does not answer our burning question about the original catastrophe, it is only too eager to tell us everything about the day after tomorrow, about the withering away of the state, and of mankind's blessed existence in a world without class, without economic oppression, without poverty, and without war. It is in the name of this promise that generations of radical and revolutionary idealists have sacrificed their lives. It is to bring about this Edenic consummation—I do want to use the word Edenic because I think it's the only right one—of man's historical destiny, that untold suffering has been visited on dissenters, heretics, saboteurs. It is because even the most brutal totalitarianism could be construed as a necessary stage of transition between class conflict and utopia, that rational men and women were prepared to serve Stalinism.

One would like to pause here and give considerable detail, because this is surely one of the clues to the mystery of why it should be that many of the most valuable young men and women in past generations, in the face of the most overwhelming evidence about the concentration camps, about perhaps the most brutal police state ever established, about the Asiatic Caesarism of Stalin, nevertheless continued to serve, to believe, and to die. If one wishes to understand the phenomenon of this kind of behaviour, it can only be in the light of a religious and messianic vision, of the great promise which says you shall wade through hell up to your eyeballs if necessary because you are on the destined, the prophetic way to the resurrection of man in the kingdom of justice. It is just because the millenarian scenario of the redemption of man and of the establishment of the kingdom of justice on earth continues to grip the human spirit (having long survived its theological premises), that every experiment in hope fires the imagination far beyond the political facts. What do I mean by experiments in hope? All of us have our own list. When I think of my own students in Cambridge in England, I have a calendar of the great moments of inner hope for them—the Prague spring before the Dubcek regime was crushed by Soviet counter-action; Chile and the Allende government; the seeming miracle of the overthrow of reaction in Portugal and in Greece. The facts are never a counter-argument. If we were to open our newspaper tomorrow morning and hear that the Portuguese coup had been a fraud, or that it was really financed by sinister forces of the Right, or that it was being overthrown, there would be grief and bitterness. But then hope would find another scenario, because we are dealing with a religious, with a theological, force.

I think we recognize in the history of Marxism each of the attributes which we cited as characteristic of a mythology in the full theological mould. We have the vision of the prophet and the canonic texts which are bequeathed to the faithful by the most important apostle. Witness the whole relation between Marx and Engels; the posthumous

9

completion of the "Kapital"; the gradual publication of the early sacred texts. We find a history of ferocious conflict between the orthodox heirs to the master and the heretics, an unbroken family of fission from the time of the Mensheviks to Trotsky and now to Mao. Each time (and this is the theological scenario) a new group of heretics breaks away; and it always says, look, we have the real message of the master; listen to us, the sacred texts have been corrupted, the Gospel is in our keeping; don't listen to the church at the centre. How familiar all this is to students of the history of Christianity. Marxism has its legends, it has its iconography, by which I mean the standard pictures of Lenin, the whole history of Lenin's life in millions of stories, tales, operas, films—even ballet. Marxism has its vocabulary. Marxism has its emblems, its symbolic gestures, just like any transcendent religious faith. It says to the believer, I want from you a total commitment. I want from you a total investment of conscience and person into my keeping. And in exchange, as does a great theology, it offers a complete explanation of man's function in biological and in social reality. Above all, it offers a contract of messianic promise concerning the future.

Personally, I must express the belief—perhaps I could put it more strongly and sadly—I must express the conviction that both the Marxist explanation of the human condition and its promise as to our future state, have been illusory. The Marxist analysis of history has shown itself to be one-sided and often grossly in violation of evidence. Crucial Marxist predictions have simply been unfulfilled, and I don't think one needs to be a technical or professional economist to know how wildly wrong Marxism has been about, for example, the pauperization of the working class or the prophecy made over and over again of the imminent cataclysmic collapse of capitalism. Remember the endless prophecies of the early Christians about the coming end of the real world, first in the year 1000, then in the year 1666.

Today one hears of extremist sects on the mountains of California looking at their mystical calendar. Over and over we find this mechanism of saying, look, we know the end is almost in sight and that the new Jerusalem will descend upon us from the heavens. Marxism, too, has predicted over and over the apocalypse of its enemies and the coming of the classless, perfect society. So on grounds of prophecy as well as on grounds of history, it has failed. Worse, where it is in power it has not brought liberation but bureaucratic terror. Already the Marxist programme for mankind is beginning to assume aspects of historical decay. Already we are beginning to look back at a great house of belief and conviction, starting up in the mid-nineteenth century, changing our world, of course—as do these great religious mythologies—but being eroded itself and crumbling at many of its vital points. Marxism, too, is beginning to look today like one of the great, empty churches.

But let us not deceive ourselves as to the tragic and pervasive force of this failure, if failure indeed it be. What was at stake was no mere technical critique of certain economic institutions; it is not over theoretical questions of investment, division of labour, or trade cycles, that generations of men and women fought, died, and killed others. The vision, the promise, the summons to total dedication and a renewal of man, were, in the full sense, messianic, religious, theological. Or to borrow the title of a celebrated book, it is "a God who failed".

Marxists like to refer to their beliefs as "scientific". They speak of the laws of history, of the scientific method of the dialectic. I suggested to you in my first talk that such claims can themselves be a part of a mythology, that they do not reflect a scientific status in any genuine sense, but rather the endeavour to inherit the defunct authority, the dogmatic certitudes, of Christian theology.

The great British philosopher and sceptic, Sir Karl Popper—so much of whose work bears on the problem of how we tell the difference between a real science and other kinds of mental activity—designates Marxism as one of the two great modern instances of what he calls a "pseudo-science"; the other pseudoscience, he tells us cheerfully, is the whole Freudian school of psychoanalysis. Here also, argues Popper, we have the professional trappings and idiom of an exact science without any of the true substance. Psychoanalytic theories, he tells us, are not subject to falsification through crucial experiment. At no stage do Freudian accounts of the structure of human consciousness and of the effects of the structure on your and my behaviour allow the kind of experimental counter-evidence which would prove them false. In the Popperian view, the absence of such a disqualification means that Freudian psychology has no status among proper scientific models.

Now we need not, I think, accept the whole of this extremely witty and acid scheme of Sir Karl's about demarcation between a science and other less respectable forms of human thought. After all, a good deal of science does in fact proceed without postulating adequate tests for self-refutation. But he has put his finger on a very real problem with respect to the nature of psychoanalysis. Far more acutely than most of his disciples, Freud was determined to give to psychoanalysis a biological foundation. His writings, his personal career, the conventions which he attempted to formulate for his followers, testify to an intense fear of becoming separated from the natural sciences. Freud dreaded—yes, I think that's the honest word—the widening gap between psychoanalysis and clinical investigation, between the psychoanalytic image of the tripartite architecture of the mind—id, ego, superego—or the dynamics of repression and sublimation on the one hand, and the neurophysiological, the biochemical treatment of mental functions, on the other. Almost until the end of his life he hoped for material, experimentally verifiable confirmation of the theories he had put forward—theories which he knew he had developed on an intuitive, introspective basis. There is in his late writings a very moving image where he speaks of the left lobe of the id, an image so moving because it shows this great longing for the solid piece of clinical evidence.

It is, I think, fair to say (and here, surely, lies the essential tragedy of the Freudian enterprise) that no such clinical, experimental confirmation has been forthcoming. Key concepts such as the libido, the castration complex, the id, remain unsupported by any direct or even analogous structures in human neurophysiology. The definition of that which could constitute a cure remains no less problematic than does the question of whether or not analysis can ever be said to have terminated. The suggestive force, the descriptive finesse of Freudian classifications and categories, are not in doubt. What is unclear is their status in regard to evidence, to control, to falsification. Increasingly, we have come to realize that Freudian models and concepts are themselves enthralling pictures, scenarios, metaphors; that they are grounded not in any external scientifically demonstrable body of fact, but in the individual genius of their founder and in local circumstance.

I put forward with hesitation, but with, I hope, some seriousness, the suggestion that the famous division of human consciousness—the id, ego, superego—has in it more than a hint of the cellar, living quarters, attic anatomy of the middle-class home in Vienna at the turn of the century. Freud's theories are not scientific in the sense of being universal, of being independent of their social-ethnic milieu, as are the theories of physics or molecular biology. They are inspired readings of, and projections from, the very special economic, familial, sexual conditions of bourgeois existence in central and western Europe between, let us say, the 1880s and the 1920s. To a degree which such famous criticisms as those of the anthropologist Malinowski soon revealed, the Freudian pattern of instinctual drive and repression does not apply to matriarchal societies or to kinship systems remote from the European norm. The evidential body for psychoanalysis is not a body of material or organic phenomena in the sense, for example, known to the neurochemist. It is a particular assemblage of linguistic and behavioural habits in a given time and place. The status of a psychoanalytic proposition is not (as Freud so persistently hoped it might be) that of a postulate in Darwin's theory of evolution. (And it was Darwin who in some ways was the model of Freud's ambitions.) Its truths are those of an intuitive, aesthetic order such as we find in philosophy and in literature. Freud's peers, his allies in his great voyage into the interior, were, as he himself came to feel, Schopenhauer, Proust, or Thomas Mann.

Now this is not to denigrate the seminal power of Freud's insights. It is a mere commonplace that these insights have exercised a formidable feedback on Western culture. Our sense of self, of our personal relations—I would almost say of the way we move inside our skin—all these have been permeated by Freudian styles. Many of Freud's conjectures have been self-fulfilling in that private and social mores have altered so as to meet psychoanalytic expectations. It is not just a nasty joke to say that so many neuroses arose after Freud had taught us to expect them. But this great enrichment of the image we have of our experience, this ability to generate objective data—because psychoanalysis almost invents its necessary patients—these do not by themselves point to a scientific status. They suggest the kind of metaphoric totality of diagnosis, the kind of symbolic scenario, which we referred to in the case of Marxism. Resolutely anti-religious as are Freud's teachings, they too, I think, constitute a form of post-theology, of surrogate or substitute theology. And theirs also is a mythological structure.

Psychoanalysis has a threefold involvement with myth. And let me try and keep these three functions as clearly distinct as I am able to. First, from the outset, Freud made use of myths and of the poetic fictive material in literature to provide crucial evidence for his theories. We will look at an example in a moment. Secondly, consciously or subconsciously— and remember Freud himself has told us to keep that difference fluid—Freud came to associate his own life work and the difficult history of the psychoanalytic movement with a mythical model. This too we will consider. Finally, in his late writings Freud developed a profoundly moving mythology of human creation and human extinction through which to make understandable, to dramatize, the conclusions which he had arrived at concerning the nature of man. These three functions or uses of the mythical do overlap and they act on each other reciprocally, but I think it is useful to keep them apart.

Let me illustrate the first from a cardinal example, indeed an example which is fundamental to the whole of Freud's model. During the late months of 1896 and in the first half of 1897 Freud accumulated material gleaned from the fantasies, day-dreams, obsession patterns of his patients. Over and over again this material seemed to point to the fact that a little girl had been seduced by her father. At first Freud was inclined to believe that this had happened. Then he began to worry—too many little girls being seduced by too many fathers, which even in degenerate Vienna of that moment didn't make sense! He begins looking for a different explanation. In a letter to his friend, to a fellow physician, Fliess, of September 21st, 1897, we see the dim of morning. He suddenly says, "this could leave open the possible explanation that sexual fantasy regularly makes use of the theme of the parents". Later in the same letter, Freud says casually, "you ask how I'm feeling. Well, I vary Hamlet's remark about ripeness—I answer to you, dear Fliess, cheerfulness is all". We stop at once. We notice a double misquotation. Of course, we notice this because Freud has told us to notice it. He is trying to quote Lear, but Hamlet is working in his searching, tensed consciousness. The problem of the Shakesperean play is acting as a catalyst—it's lashing around in his mind.

On the 15th October comes the Copernican hour in the history of the whole psychoanalytic movement. "Being entirely honest with oneself is a good exercise. One idea of general value has occurred to me. I have found love of the mother, jealousy of the father, in my own case too, and now believe it to be a general phenomenon of all early childhood. If that is the case, the power of *Oedipus Rex* of Sophocles, in spite of all the objections to the inexorable fate in the play, becomes perfectly intelligible. Every member of the audience becomes Oedipus in his fantasy, and this dream fulfilment played out in reality causes everybody to recoil in horror when the full measure of repression which separates his infantile traits from his present state is revealed. Now another idea passes through my head. Isn't this the root of *Hamlet*? I'm not thinking of Shakespeare's conscious intentions, but am supposing rather that he was impelled to write

16

it by a real event, because his own unconscious understood that of his hero. How can one explain the hysteric Hamlet's phrase 'So conscience doth make cowards of us all', [and I pause—he's again misquoting a little] and Hamlet's hesitation to avenge his father by killing his uncle when he himself so casually sends his courtiers to their death and despatches Laertes so quickly? How better than by the torment roused in him by the obscure memory that he himself had meditated the same deed against his father because of passionate desire for his mother? Use every man after his desert and who shall escape whipping? His conscience is his unconscious feeling of guilt."

Now the point I want to underline, and it can be made throughout Freud's mature work, is that the ancient myths, the fiction, the novel, the poem, the play, the scenario proposed by the novelist or dramatist, are not adduced as a more or less contingent parallel. Nor are they cited only in illustration. At the core of Freud's theoretic model, they provide indispensable validation. Where one might expect a supporting body of clinical-statistical evidence, the recital of a large number of cases, Freud offers the "proof"—I put the word in quotes—of myth and of literature. This happens again and again. When he published his conjectures about the Oedipus complex, the cries throughout the so-called civilized world were horrifying. Pursued also in his private life at the time by the accusation of being a sex-mad charlatan, who had forever sullied the innocence of families and despoiled little boys and girls of their purity in the sight of God, Freud answered in a characteristic way: "Why am I attacked? The proof of what I am saying is abundantly present in the great poets of the past. In *Oedipus*, Jocasta proclaims 'Before this in dreams, too, as well as in oracles, many a man has slept with his own mother.' And in Diderot's great novel, *Le Neveu de Rameau*, I read 'If the child—le petit sauvage—were left to himself, if he preserved all his foolishness and combined the violent passions of a man of thirty

17

with the lack of reason of a child in the cradle, he'd wring his father's neck and jump into bed with his mother.'" It is precisely at the great crisis point in his thought that the distance from a scientific mode of argument and evidencing is most clear, and that we notice the affinity to a religious or religious-metaphysical proceeding as, for example, in Plato. The demonstration for Freud of the reality of the universality of his therapeutic metaphors, such as the Oedipus complex, are themselves metaphoric constructs, archetypal dramas, bodied forth and transmitted in myths.

The second aspect is much more difficult to handle, and I am sharply aware of the very provisional quality of what I want to suggest to you. Remember that we saw that Marx identified his mission, his dramatic function in human history, with that of Prometheus, the bringer of the torch of rebellion and of truth to enslave man. In the case of Sigmund Freud there would appear to have been a great measure of self-identification with, or self-projection onto, the figure of Moses. There have been detailed studies of Freud's own somewhat enigmatic essay or monograph on the *Moses* of Michelangelo, that overwhelming statue which literally overcame him when he first saw it in the shadows, in the corner of that little dark church in Rome, San Pietro in Vincoli. Freud seeing it, fainted. As his professional situation became both more eminent and more controversial, as both notoriety and solitude deepened around his self-consciousness, Freud seems to have analogized between the Mosaic wanderings and the advance of the psychoanalytic movement. He too was a great leader, severe, unyielding, destined to lead mankind, or some significant portion of it at least, to a promised land of rationality, of psychic equilibrium and scientific truth. He too was seeking to reform a small, recalcitrant band of the faithful into a great international movement.

Like Moses, his battle was one which had, at all times, to be sustained on two fronts: against the Gentiles, the

Philistines, the false sages who would entrap the science of the mind in censorship and superstition, and against the vacillations, the recalcitrance, the treason, of his own followers. The latter was always—he tells us this himself—the worse of the two battles. He could handle the Philistines and the attackers and the censors but not the desperate betrayals of those closest to him. One after another, like Aaron, like Korah and his rout, the most faithful rebelled, split away from the founder, established rival schools. Alfred Adler, Otto Rank, Wilhelm Reich, Jung—rebellion after rebellion, betrayal after betrayal, by the most gifted, by those nearest to him, by the elected sons. Yet whatever the personal suffering and aloneness of the leader, the movement must march forward—refusing compromise and guarding the law in its original purity. Through the desert of ridicule and active enmity to the threshold of victory. Indeed, vexed as he was in his personal end, in exile, wracked with physical pain, Freud knew that psychoanalysis had become a world phenomenon. He suspected that America might be its promised land, and he was fully aware that his name had passed into the household of language.

It is, I believe, in the perspective of this identification, intermittent no doubt, with the talismanic figure and sage of Moses, that we must view one of Freud's very last works, the study of *Moses and Monotheism*. The puzzle, of course, is this: why should Freud, so intimately involved with the person of Moses, make of the begetter of Israel and of modern monotheism an Egyptian? I have never seen a plausible explanation. My own is only tentative. As he wrote the book in 1938 Freud could see the storm of Nazism gathering over European Jewry. Rightly, he identified the peculiar moral genius and demandingness of Judaic monotheism, of Judaic legalism, with Moses. By making of Moses an Egyptian, a leader who had come to the Jews from outside, Freud may, unconsciously, have sought to divert from the Jewish people the new wave of Gentile hatred.

Such displacement was, to be sure, illusory. But it points again to the mythological, myth-making fabric of the Freudian method.

The third aspect concerns the generation of myths. In psychoanalysis, as in Marxism, there is a mystery of original sin. But unlike that of Marx, Freud's account is specific. He tells of the patricide enacted in the primal horde, of the castration and/or murder of the father figure by the sons. Humanity, says Freud, bears the mark of this primal crime. From it flows the long history of adjustment between instinctual drive and social repression, between indiscriminate sexuality and family order, and this adjustment is far less than perfect. *Civilization and its Discontents*, one of his last works, offers an ironic, desolate diagnosis of the strains, suppressions, distortions, suffered by the psyche in the process of its adjustment to the economies of ordered society. Pondering the seemingly inherent unhappiness of the human species, meshed in a dialectic of biological and social thrusts and constraints, Freud now advances deeper into the mythological.

The little book, *Beyond the Pleasure Principle*, is one of the most extraordinary documents of the history of the Western tragic imagination. It formulates (and remember, it is only very rare individuals of genius who can do so) a myth of the meaning of life as comprehensive, as metaphorically authoritative, as those that have come down to us from ancient, collective sources. Two deities, two gods, two overwhelming agencies, govern and divide our being, said Freud. Love and death, Eros and Thanatos. The conflict between them determines the rhythms of existence, of procreation, of somatic and psychic evolution. But finally—the contrary to all intuitive, instinctive expectations, to all our hopes—it is not Eros, not love, but Thanatos who is the stronger, who is closer to the roots of man. What the species strives for, finally, is not survival and perpetuation, but repose, perfect inertness. In Freud's visionary programme, the explosion of organic life, which has led to human evolution, was a kind of tragic anomaly, almost a fatal exuberance. It has brought with it untold pain and ecological waste. But this detour of life and consciousness will sooner or later end. An internal entropy is at work. A great quietness will return to creation as life reverts to the natural condition of the inorganic. The consummation of the libido lies in death.

Freud *insisted* that these were imagistic speculations, that they did not belong to his scientific labours, but to what he himself called the "metapsychology" of an aging man in a community overshadowed by the recurrence of world war and the more particular terror of a holocaust of the Jews. But the scientific and the mythological do interpenetrate with each other much earlier. The myth of the murder in the primal horde is vital to the Freudian analysis of the tensions of consciousness in modern man. The model of a dialectic of Eros and Thanatos is implicit in Freud's whole theory of instinct and rationality. *Beyond the Pleasure Principle* is, unquestionably, a metaphoric speculation; but its depth, its sombre conviction, derive from the whole unfolding and logic of Freud's theses. It is the crowning act in Freud's unbroken attempt to reconcile man to a godless reality, to make this reality endurable by suggesting a final release from it. It is in this sense that both the Marxist and the Freudian blueprints for man are scenarios of deliverance—Prometheus, Moses, liberators, deliverers, both. But whereas Marx intimates an Edenic condition free of necessity and of conflict, Freud knows that such freedom would be tantamount to the repose of death.

In both *Totem and Taboo*, an earlier book, and *Moses and Monotheism*, Freud explicitly invokes the notion of a collective inheritance of primal memories. He speaks of the transmission of archetypal experiences and traumas via the unconscious of the human race. The same idea is, of course, implicit in the meta-psychology of *Beyond the Pleasure Princi-*

ple. There is until now, no neuro-chemical, no neuro-physiological warrant whatever for this audacious conjecture. In fact the notion of inherited or racial archetypal memories goes totally against everything which molecular biology suggests as a plausible account of the genetic mechanism. It is a piece of mythology of controlling metaphor as vital to the agnostic world view of Freud as is the parallel metaphor of sin to the world view of theology. For Freud, this inheritance of the archetypal remembrance of man's prime plays the same role as the fall of man, man's disobedience of God in Pauline theology.

Now, as is well known, the concept of a collective unconscious in which dreams, memories, seminal images are embedded, are transmitted over generations, nay, over millenia. This is crucial to the psychology of Jung and to his whole theory of archetype. As the recent publication of the Freud-Jung letters, which had been awaited for so long, shows, the bitter break between the two men had complex and cumulative motives. A very different emphasis on the role of sexuality, on the nature of the therapeutic process, was doubtless among the most aggravating. But the coincidence of views between Freud and Jung on the inheritance of archetypal psychic material and images does suggest to me that the quarrel between Freudian and Jungian theories is not, at every point, an entirely genuine one. Or, to put it more precisely, it suggests that there were in Freud's view of Jung's rebellion, of Jung's betrayal, elements themselves opaque to him.

Freudian psychoanalysis was resolved to remove from the human psyche the infantile illusions—that's his own phrase—of religion. He was going to liberate man from the childishness of metaphysical beliefs. Jung's psychology, of course, does not only draw on religious experience for many of its main categories, but sees in religion a necessary, evolving component in the history and health of the human soul. Thus the Freudian quarrel with the Jungian model is, I think, in part, a dispute between agnosticism and transcendent belief, and on a much deeper level, a duel between a new mythology, a surrogate belief, and a system which wants to restore the ancient rival gods. Let me quote from one of these very newly published letters. Jung is writing to Freud in the early days of their understanding.

> "I think, dear Dr. Freud," he says, "we must give psychoanalysis time to infiltrate into people from many centres, to revivify among intellectuals a feeling for symbol and myth. Ever so gently we want to transform Christ back into the soothsaying god of the vine, which he was, and in this way absorb those ecstatic instinctual forces of Christianity for the one purpose of making the cult and the sacred myth what they once were—a drunken feast of joy where man regains the ethos and holiness of an animal. That was the beauty and purpose of classical religion."

It is a very curious statement. I think it explains something of the severity and personal drama of the break between the two men. Jung was saying to Freud no less than this: let us bring back the ancient gods.

Like orthodox Marxism, classical Freudian psychoanalysis is already receding into history. No analyst today meets patients anything like those described in Freud's own cases. Clinical support remains problematic. The movement has splintered into dozens of bitterly rival churches. The liberation initiated by Freud in regard to our awareness of sexuality, of the autonomous needs of children, in regard to psychopathology and mental illness, has been very considerable. Because Freud lived and worked, we do breathe more freely, both in our private and social existence. But the issue was a much larger one. Freud sought to banish the archaic shadows of irrationalism, of faith in the supernatural. His promise, like that of Marx, was a promise of light. It has not been fulfilled. On the contrary.

Early on in *Tristes Tropiques*, his famous philosophic auto-biography, Claude Lévi-Strauss, the French anthropologist, tells of the decisive influence of Marx and Freud on his own vocation and on his own methods. Lévi-Strauss tells us that he sees in Marxism and in psychoanalysis two modes of radical understanding and reconstitution which he compares with those used in geology.

The Marxist analysis of French society and social and class conflict, as put forward in Marx's book *The Eighteenth Brumaire of Louis Bonaparte*, the Freudian case study, these are analogous penetrations below the appearance, below the surface of phenomena. Like the geologist, the Marxist social thinker and the Freudian analyst uncover the dynamic levels of stress, the sedimentation, which determine the contour of the landscape. Both systems of explanation, moreover, again just like those of the geologist, go in depth. They go in depth structurally and historically; their mapping of social or psychic strata constitute a history. They tell us how this piece of earth was produced: Why the mountains and valleys? How did the rivers come to be dug? They tell us how the surface features—social institutions, behaviour, speech patterns—have evolved, and how they are the necessary end-product of a long process in time.

With a high degree of self-consciousness and with a confidence which is sometimes a little awesome, M. Lévi-Strauss tells us that he will complete, and, by clear inference, correct and improve upon, the labours of Marx and of Freud. It is this explicit combinatorial design which underwrites the claims to totality in his use of the word "anthropology". Like no "anthropologist" before him, with the possible exception of Rousseau, Claude Lévi-Strauss employs this word in its complete etymological sense: anthropology, properly understood, is no less than the exhaustive "science of man"—*la science de l'homme.* You and I are to hear in the word the complete play of values and connotations associated with the Greek root "logos"—which as we all know is such a difficult word, ranging from "spirit" and "ordering speech" to "logic" and, perhaps, to "incarnate mystery" in the way it is used in the Fourth Gospel. An anthropologist, if he is not to be a mere ethnographer or collector of exotica, is, says Lévi-Strauss, no less than a "scientist of man" to whose comprehensive model of the nature of human life the Marxist investigation of social forces and the Freudian mapping of consciousness are preliminary. It is a majestic claim; but only if we bear it plainly in mind can we grasp the scope, the unifying impulse, of Lévi-Strauss's great enterprise.

In trying to say something adequate concerning that enterprise, my disqualifications are all too obvious. The format of these talks allows us only a limited time. Much of the material is technical and could be debated only by Lévi-Strauss's professional colleagues. At key points, moreover, the texts are elusive and there is a certain degree of orchestral rhetoric, inseparable from Lévi-Strauss's great genius as a writer. But to anyone concerned with the postulate and merits of the great mythologies which have attempted to fill the vacuum left by religion, Lévi-Strauss's work is of cardinal interest. Here, indeed, is a creator of myths, a mythographer, an inventor of legends, to whom the notion of a complete, total mythology is absolutely central.

If time allowed, I would want to sketch the background of this centrality. The very distant precedent is the Italian thinker, Vico, of the late seventeenth century and early eighteenth, whose *New Science* for the first time said that the myths, the stories of Greek antiquity, the fables, had a vital nucleus of social and psychological history. Other models lay closer at hand in Michelet, in Victor Hugo, and in Wagner. Hugo's *Legende des siecles*, Wagner's *Götterdämmerung* have their very precise counterpart in Lévi-Strauss's *Pensée sauvage* and *Mythologiques*. Even Lévi-Strauss's prose style has that orchestral texture so reminiscent of the epic arts of the nineteenth century. But this would be a subject in its own right.

For Claude Lévi-Strauss, myths are, quite simply, the instruments of man's survival as a thinking and social species. It is through myths that man makes sense of the world, that he experiences it in some coherent fashion, that he confronts its irremediably contradictory, divided, alien presence. Man is enmeshed in primal contradictions between being and non-being, male and female, youth and age, light and dark, the edible and the toxic, the mobile and the inert. He cannot, says Lévi-Strauss, resolve these formidable, clashing antitheses by purely rational processes. He is at either pole of conceivable time, confronted with the mystery of his origins and then confronted with the mystery of his extinction. Chaos is co-existent with seemingly exquisite symmetries. Myths alone are able to articulate these universal antinomies, to find figurative explanations for the divided situation of man in nature. Man is, in Lévi-Strauss's view, a mythopoetic primate (it's a difficult phrase but we don't have a better one), a primate capable of manufacturing, creating myths, and through these enduring the contradictory, insoluble tenor of his fate. He alone can construct, modulate, and give emotional adherence to the mytho-logical (a necessary hyphen), the mythical and the logical, the logical inside the myth.

There is an Hassidic parable which tells us that God created man so that man might tell stories. This telling of stories is, according to Lévi-Strauss, the very condition of our being. The alternative would be total inertia or the eclipse of reason. The mediative, ordering capacity of myths, their ability to "encode"—another Lévi-Strauss word—to give coherent expression to reality, points to a profound harmonic accord between the inner logic of the brain and the structure of the external world. "When the mind processes the empirical data which it receives previously processed by the sense organs, it goes on working out structurally that which at the outset was already structural. And it can only do so inasmuch as the mind, the body to which the mind belongs, and the things which body and mind perceive, are part and parcel of one and the same reality." The codes through which these perceptions are transmitted and understood are, suggests Lévi-Strauss, binary. That's again a technical word, but not difficult for us to understand. He says that everything that matters comes in sets of two. Thus we have the relations and interactions of what he calls "the great pairings". For example, affirmation and negation, which really means in simple language, yes and no; organic and inorganic; left and right; before and after. Lévi-Strauss suggests that the symmetries of the nervous system and the hemispheric architecture of the human cortex—the two halves of our brain—seem to be an active reflection of this binary structure of reality.

Of all the fundamental polarities which structure the destiny and the science of man, the most important, according to Lévi-Strauss, is that of Nature and Culture (he usually spells these two words with capital letters). In the inmost of his being and history, man is a divided composite of biological and socially-culturally acquired elements. It is the interplay between biological constraints on the one hand, and social-cultural variables on the other, which determines our condition. That interplay is at every point dynamic because the environment, as it impinges on human biology, is itself modified by man's social and cultural activities. But the

27

binary set, Nature/Culture, also points to an essential ambiguity, even tragedy, in the genesis of human consciousness.

We have seen in the two previous talks, that both Marx and Freud took over from religion and from systematic theology the inference of original sin, of a fall of man—though neither mythology is really completely specific as to the occasion of this disaster. Lévi-Strauss is specific. Necessary as it was, imprinted as it must have been in the genetic code and evolutionary potential of the human race, our transition from a natural to a cultural state was also a destructive step, and one that has left scars on both the human psyche and the organic world.

Lévi-Strauss clarifies his meaning by reference to two myths—and it is surely acutely witty or worrying for us that the two myths Lévi-Strauss chooses should be precisely those which Marx and Freud respectively had picked as their main emblems. You remember that to Marx, Prometheus was the symbol of revolutionary intelligence, of the rebellion of intellect against ignorance and arbitrary tyranny. Freud lights on the erotic intimations in the theme. He tells of the rapture of fire in a hollow phallic reed, of the sexually laden symbolism of the devouring bird, and the daily renewal of Prometheus's potency. Lévi-Strauss's reading is totally different. The Promethean appropriation of fire to human needs and wishes encodes the catastrophic step whereby man acquired control over the principal factors in his biological setting. Having stolen fire, man can now have light during hours of darkness; having hunted his prey, with fire he can now preserve the meat in smoked or cooked form and need not eat it on the spot; having fire from Prometheus, he can bring warmth into his dwelling, thus overcoming constraints of winter. The control of fire is the premise of social-cultural progress, surely. But it has been achieved, says Lévi-Strauss, at a formidable cost. Possessing a hearth and the art of cooking, man has broken with the animal world, with the immediate shared relationships of consumer to food. Having altered the binary polarities of light and dark, of heat and cold, of night and day, man finds himself in an unnatural power-relation to his environment and to his own animal origins. This ambiguity is symbolized by Prometheus's half human, half divine status. The divorce from the natural order brought on by his theft of fire (and the notion of theft *is* primal to the legend) is punished by Prometheus's isolation and by the assaults on him of the eagle.

Go back to the great myths which have engaged the human imagination and whose thematic elements turn up in all languages and ethnic groups, says Lévi-Strauss, and you will find at their roots some trace of man's cultural break with the natural world, and of the deep discomforts which this break has left in our souls. Discomfort—Freud's word was *Unbehagen*, Marx's word *alienation*. The Oedipus myth is another case in point—and Lévi-Strauss's gloss on Oedipus is an undisguised critique and correction of his great rival, Freud. Lévi-Strauss fixes on just those motifs which Freud's decipherment neglects. Oedipus's answer to the riddle of the Sphinx, you remember, was the word "man". That is one feature which Freud pays no attention to. And the second feature which Freud does not even mention, is the fact that Oedipus limps. And it is precisely these features that excite Lévi-Strauss.

As Lévi-Strauss reads it, we have here yet another myth, another structural ordering of man's divided being. Once all of us were walkers or runners on all fours. Man then compelled his backbone to be erect. We now move on two limbs only, we dominate the landscape, we dominate the animal species. But no less than the rape of fire, this sovereign singularity has left us, quite literally, off balance. The hominids, as it were, limped into the state of humanity. Thus the incest theme in the Oedipus story is not, as Freud would have it, a dramatization of suppressed infantile sexuality. It points to the all-decisive coming into being of defined kinship categories. Oedipus assumes the burden of the transition of the human species from indiscriminate couplings, as in so many animal kinds, to the economic and generational continuities of a familial code.

The prohibition of certain degrees of incest determines, and indeed defines, man's identity as a social-historical consciousness. It is wholly inseparable from the human speech evolution. And here Lévi-Strauss makes one of his inspired guesses. He says that we can only prohibit that which our vocabulary and grammar are exact and rich enough to designate. In other words, not until you have a sufficiently rich sentence structure and enough words to define the third cousin four times removed of the mother's uncle can you have incest and kinship rules. So that grammar, in a way, is a necessary condition for basic moral law. Kinship rules are, literally, the semantics of human existence. But once again, the break with Nature, the advance into Culture, has been one of estrangement from the environment and from the animal in ourselves. Language is the necessary condition of human excellence, but man can neither communicate with his animal kindred nor cry to them for help.

Even these abbreviated, simplified examples should indicate something of the breadth of Lévi-Strauss's "anthropo-logy"—always that hyphen—and of his own mythopoetic instincts. Formally, his work elucidates the structure of meaning, the transformational rules, the relations to ritual and to development of written narrative, of some 800 American-Indian myths. It is through this elucidation that Lévi-Strauss seeks to establish the principles of correspondence which connect man's psychosomatic evolution, the structure of our brain, the nature of language, and the physical environment. But though he likes to define himself merely as a student of myths, Lévi-Strauss is, in fact, a creator of mythology, and the comparison with Frazer's role in *The Golden Bough* is at once obvious and, from the point of view of Lévi-Strauss's technical status in the field, somewhat disturbing. If I do not mistake his meaning, Lévi-Strauss has been voicing a prophetic vision of apocalypse as vengeful, as persuasive, as any conceived since the Book of Revelation and the millenarian panics of the tenth century.

As I say this, I touch on what is, of course, a very worrying problem—the question again: Are we dealing with a scientific, systematic body of thought? Being an outsider, it would be entirely impertinent for me to do more than refer to the differences which now divide Lévi-Strauss's conception of what an anthropologist does, from that conception in the lives and professional activity of his academic colleagues. To them he is a spinner of purple fantasies. He, on the contrary, regards them as people so wretchedly unimaginative that they actually have to go and sit in tents or savannahs or deserts, looking at moribund natives, in order to find out what they already knew was there. I do not think we should try and judge.

From our point of view what is fascinating is to follow in Lévi-Strauss the evolution of a great post-religious, pseudo-theological explanation of man. It goes something like this. The fall of man did not, at one stroke, eradicate all the vestiges of the Garden of Eden. Great spaces of primeval nature and of animal life did persist. The eighteenth-century travellers succumbed to a kind of premeditated illusion when they thought to have found innocent races of men in the paradise of the South Seas or in the great forests of the New World. But their idealizations had a certain validity. Having existed, as it were, outside history, having abided by primordial social and mental usages, possessing a profound intimacy with plant and with animal, primitive men *did* embody a more natural condition. Their cultural divorce from nature had of course occurred hundreds and thousands of years ago, but it was less drastic than that of the white man: to be precise, their cultural modes, their rituals, myths, taboos, techniques of food-gathering, were calculated to assuage nature, to comfort her, to live with her, to make the break between nature and culture less savage, less dominant.

Coming upon these shadows of the remnants of Eden, Western man set out to destroy them. He slaughtered countless guiltless peoples. He clawed down the forests, he charred the savannah. Then his fury of waste turned on the animal species. One after another of these was hounded into extinction or into the factitious survival of the zoo. This devastation was often deliberate: it resulted directly from military conquest, from economic exploitation, from the imposition of uniform technologies on native life-styles. Millions perished or lost their ethnic heritage and identity. Some observers put at twenty million the number of victims in the Congo alone, from the start of Belgian rule. Languages, each of which had encoded a unique vision of the world, were steam-rollered into oblivion. The egret and the whale were hunted almost to annihilation. Often also, destruction came accidentally or even out of benevolence. The gifts which the white man had brought—medical gifts, material, institutional—proved fatal to their recipients. Whether he came to conquer or to proselytize, to exploit or to medicate, Western man brought devastation. Possessed, as it were, by some archetypal rage at his own exclusion from the Garden of Paradise, by some torturing remembrance of that disgrace, we have scoured the earth for vestiges of Eden and laid them waste wherever we have found them.

Lévi-Strauss's analysis of this desolation has a special, ironic poignancy. For the anthropologist himself has played his own ambivalent part in the affair of destruction. The notion of travelling to far places in order to study alien peoples and cultures, is unique to Western man; it springs from the predatory genius of the Greeks; no primitive peoples have ever come to study us. This is, on the one hand, a disinterested, intellectually inspired impulse. It is one of our glories. But it is, on the other, part and parcel of exploitation. No native community survives intact after the anthropologist's visit—however skilful, however self-effacing, however tactful he may be. The Western obsession with inquiry, with analysis, with the classification of all living forms, is itself a mode of subjugation, of psychological and technical mastery. Fatally, analytic thought will adulterate or destroy the vitality of its object. Lévi-Strauss's *Tristes Tropiques* turns on this melancholy paradox.

With the years, Lévi-Strauss's visionary anger has intensified. The ravage of the vegetable and animal orders in the name of technological progress, the exploitation of a major part of humanity for the benefit of a few, the scarcely examined Western assumption of superiority over the so-called primitive, underdeveloped communities—all these fill Lévi-Strauss with contemptuous loathing. The political barbarism of the twentieth century, such phenomena as the holocaust and the nuclear arms race, seem to Lévi-Strauss to be no accident. They are the direct correlatives of the white man's murderous treatment of ecology. Having ravaged what little remained of Eden (and this is the logic of Lévi-Strauss's punitive metaphor or myth), the Western predator must now turn on himself.

We can surely answer "yes", but we are now conscious of the ruin we have brought. We can say that the more thoughtful of Western men, and the young in particular, are trying to save the natural environment, to rescue animal species, to protect what pitiful islands of virgin earth are still to be found. Too late, says Lévi-Strauss, much too late. Our very experiments in salvage—witness the Indian reservations in Amazonia—bring with them new dislocations, new erosions. Where economic-political interests are at stake—be it in the whaling industry, in the Alaskan pipe line, or in the emancipation of New Guinea—cynicism and destruction will prevail. We are, says Lévi-Strauss, in consequence, doomed. Anthropology, the science of man, will culminate, he says, in "entropology". In French the pun is perfect, you can't tell the two words apart—anthropologie—entropologie. It will culminate in the science of entropy, the science of extinction. This black pun leads to a culminating image of the earth, devoid of humanity, cleansed of the garbage of human greed and self-destruction, whirling cold and void in empty space. I would like to quote the passage in full. It comes at the end of volume 4 of Lévi-Strauss's *Mythologiques*, and may I quote it in French, as we are, after all, together in a Canadian context. Also the rhythm and splendour of this passage almost defy translation:

* L'opposition fondamentale, génératrice de toutes les autres qui foisonnent dans les mythes et dont ces quatre tomes ont dressé l'inventaire, est celle même qu'énonce Hamlet sous la forme d'une encore trop crédule alternative. Car entre l'être et le non-être, il n'appartient pas à l'homme de choisir. Un effort mental consubstantiel à son histoire, et qui ne cessera qu'avec son effacement de la scène de l'univers, lui impose d'assumer les deux évidences contradictoires dont le heurt met sa pensée en branle et, pour netraliser leur opposition, engendre une série illimitée d'autres distinctions binaires qui, sans jamais résoudre cette antinomie première, ne font, à des échelles de plus réduites, que la reproduire et la perpétuer: réalité de l'être, que l'homme éprouve au plus profond de lui-même comme seule capable de donner raison et sens à ses gestes quotidiens, à sa vie morale et sentimentale a, à ses choix politiques, à son engagement dans le monde social et naturel, à ses entreprises pratiques et à ses conquêtes scientifiques; mais en même temps, réalité du non-être dont l'intuition accompagne indissolublement l'autre puis-qu'il incombe à l'homme de vivre et lutter, penser et croire, garder surtout courage, sans que jamais le quitte la certitude adverse, qu'il n'était pas présent autrefois sur la terre et qu'il ne sera pas toujours, et qu'avec sa disparition inéluctable de la surface d'une planète elle aussi vouée à la mort, ses labeurs, ses peines, ses joies, ses espoirs et ses œuvres deviendront comme s'ils n'avaient pas existé, nulle conscience n'étant plus là pour préserver fût-ce le souvenir de ces mouvements éphémeres sauf, par quelques traits vites effacés d'un monde au visage désormais impassible, le constat abrogé qu'ils eurent lieu c'est-à-dire rien.

* The fundamental alternative, the alternative which generates all those other opposing sets which crowd myths and of which these four volumes have been an

inventory, is that set forth by Hamlet, though in too credulous a form. It is not for man to choose between being and non-being. He is compelled, by a mental stress which is incarnate in his history and which will not cease until his own disappearance from the universe, to take upon himself these two contradictory alternatives. It is the clash between being and non-being which sets human thought in motion. It is the attempt to reconcile this inherent contradiction which, in turn, generates a limitless series of further binary distinctions which, without ever reconciling the primal antithesis, only reproduce it and perpetutate it on an ever diminishing scale. There is the reality of being which man experiences in his inmost depths as being alone capable of affording rationality and meaning to his daily acts, to his moral and emotional life, to his political choices, to his implication in the social and natural world, to his practical enterprises and scientific conquests. But there is, at the same time, the reality of non-being, whose perception is indivisible from that of being, since it is man's lot to live and struggle, think and believe, above all, keep steadfast, without ever losing the destructive certainty that he was not, in times past, present on this earth, that he will not endure forever, and that with his ineluctable disappearance from the surface of a planet itself destined to extinction, his labours, his pains, his joys, his hopes, and his accomplished works shall become as if they had never been. No consciousness will survive to preserve, be it no more than a remembrance of man's ephemeral doings, except by the token of a few rapidly effaced traces. Swept from a world whose features will thenceforth be expressionless and perfectly indifferent, these will have been nothing but a brief testimony that such doings did occur—in short, they will be nothing.

Listeners to these first three talks will have observed that there is, between the three mythologies we have looked at so far, what could be called a genetic link. It would require extreme discriminatory finesse and a scope beyond the present for me to assess contrastively and in depth, the Judaism of Marx, of Freud, and of Lévi-Strauss. Notoriously, Marx turned on his own ethnic-spiritual past. He came to produce a virulent text on the Jewish question, identifying Judaism with the vices of capitalism and calling, quite literally, for a final solution in terms of complete assimilation. The extremity of this proposal does, to be sure, suggest the depth of Marx's personal malaise in regard to his own status. Freud's attitudes were, as we have seen with reference to his treatment of the Moses theme, complex and, very probably, subconsciously motivated. Profoundly Jewish in his temperament, Jewish in his style of feeling and private life, he endeavoured to give to the psychoanalytical movement a larger ethnic basis, a respectability in the Gentile world. In the Preface to the Hebrew edition of *Totem and Taboo* in

1930, Freud described himself—and I quote—"as completely estranged from the religion of my fathers". But he went on—and I quote again—"If asked, 'What is left to you that is Jewish?' I would have to reply, 'A very great deal and probably the essence.' " By which he seems to have meant, the ideal of intellectual pursuit and of high moral seriousness. So far as I am aware, Lévi-Strauss has not pronounced himself on the issue; indeed he seems studiously to avoid it. His very insistence on the fact that the holocaust has no privileged status, either historically or metaphysically, that it is only a part of the general structure of massacre and extinction, shows a wish to distance himself from any Jewish particularity. I have heard him speak with disdain about those who seek to separate the holocaust in the Second World War from that continuity of massacre of human peoples, animal species, and natural forms, which in his great myth of vengeance is the principal guilt of modern man. Bitterly he will say that, of all men, the Jew should be the one most profoundly alert to, aware of, the universality of murder that surrounds him.

Nevertheless, there are specific Judaic aspects, indeed marked ones, in each of the three cases. Marx's utopian messianism, his rage for justice, his conception of the drama and logic of history, have strong roots in the prophetic and Talmudic traditions. Marx's promissory vision, which we compared to Isaiah, of the exchange of love for love, of trust for trust, his promise that history is finally rational, that it has a design and that it is a design of human liberation, these have their profoundly rich precedent and parallel in every aspect of Jewish thought. Freud's relentless intellectuality, the pessimism and severity of his ethics, his unswerving trust in the power of the word, these too relate to key aspects of Jewish sensibility. Only a man of his particular background would have believed as deeply as he did, even in the face of mounting barbarism, in the supremacy of the human word over ignorance and death and destruction. He was supremely, in the rabbinical sense, an interpreter of texts, a creator of parables. In Lévi-Strauss there is the obsessive sense of retribution, of man's failure to observe his contractual responsibilities to creation. We have never in modern times had a more powerful, a more explicit, reading of man's breach of covenant with the mystery of creation, and of his own borrowed being in a world which he should guard and preserve, in a garden which was his to cultivate and not to destroy.

But I have a more general, structural feature in mind. Here are three great mythologies devised to explain the history of man, the nature of man, and our future. That of Marx ends in a promise of redemption; that of Freud in a vision of homecoming to death; that of Lévi-Strauss in an apocalypse brought on by human evil and human waste. All three are rational mythologies claiming a normative, scientific status. All three stem from a shared metaphor of original sin. Can it be altogether accidental that these three visionary constructs—two of which, Marxism and Freud, have already done so much to change Western, and indeed, world history—should derive from a Jewish background? Is there not a real logic in the fact that these surrogates to a moribund Christian theology and account of history, that these attempts to replace a dying Christianity, should have come from those whose own legacy Christianity had done so much to supplant?

The first three talks in this series have not been altogether on the light side. Nor will the last be. So it is time for a break. But although the material I want to touch on now is inherently ludicrous, the economic prodigality which it entails, the waste of human hopes and emotions which it generates, do make it difficult for me to "keep my cool". The cults of unreason, the organized hysterias, the obscurantism which have become so important a feature of Western sensibility and behaviour during these past decades, are comical and often trivial to a degree; but they represent a failure of maturity, a self-demeaning, which are, in essence, tragic.

The phenomena I have in mind are so widespread, diverse, and interleaved that it is almost impossible in the format available to us, to do more than give a few shorthand indications. But the general fact is plain: in terms of money and of time spent, of the number of men and women involved to a greater or lesser degree, in terms of the literature produced and of institutional ramifications, ours is the psychological and the social climate most infected by superstition, by irrationalism, of any since the decline of the Middle Ages and, perhaps, even since the time of the crisis in the Hellenistic world. A classification of the relevant frauds and aberrations would be useful, as were the medieval compendia of Satanism and maleficence. But it is entirely beyond my competence, or my stomach; so let me suggest some broad, imprecise rubrics.

Statistics, admittedly provisional, tell us that astrology is now a business running into something of the order of twenty-five million dollars per annum in Western industrial societies. The investment represented by astrological pursuits in the third world and in the emergent, semi-technological communities of Asia is, most likely, past accurate computation. The literature of astrology floods the book stalls; only a very few quality newspapers now appear without a daily or weekly astrological column. Periodicals, ranging from trash to the most elegant, run weekly or monthly horoscopes. At a rough count, the number of practising astrologers in the United States exceeds by a factor of three the total number of men and women affiliated with professional bodies in physics and in chemistry. Intensities of individual credulity modulate all the way from the totally obedient—adult human beings who stay away from work, who clamber into bed when the stars are in a threatening configuration—to the mildly embarrassed, self-deprecating murmur of elegant souls who "don't really believe it all" but feel there might be something in it. "After all, don't sunspots affect the magnetic fields, my dear, and cosmic ray incidence surround the earth?" The inferred analogy happens to be absolute nonsense, but never mind that.

Now go up the scale of inanity, and you come to the astral or galactic. Unidentified flying objects have been observed in lit clusters circling, hovering above the planet Earth. Sober pilots have recorded sightings in the blue deeps of the jet stream. Aerodynamic saucers have given amiable chase to automobiles hurrying home on highways in Arizona or New South Wales. But these are only trifles. UFOs have landed, leaving egg-shaped burn marks and flattened grass. In a number of cases, bizarre but benign beings have stepped out and taken Earthlings into brief custody. They have voiced consoling or monitory sentiments about man's future, his political destiny, his ecological salvation. They have entered into collaborative concourse with certain gifted human individuals, bestowing on them powers of clairvoyance and psychokinetic action (or so Mr. Uri Geller's biographer assures us).

Do you doubt these current visitations? Surely you cannot question the "overwhelming evidence" of extra-terrestial callers in the past? Just look around you: at the rock drawings in the Sahara or the Kalahari with their seeming astronomical markings and mysterious silhouettes of figures with pointed heads; at the odd criss-cross patterns and hatchings apparently incised in high Andean valleys, lineaments only fully perceptible from the air; at the skull of a Neanderthal man pierced by an allegedly spherical, metallic missile; at enigmatically sited dolmens and menhirs in otherwise trackless landscapes; at bits of putatively undecipherable writing or pictograms older than the Easter Island script or the runes of Mohenjo-Daro. Look wherever you will in ancient mythologies or, for that matter, at the account of how the sons of God came to the daughters of men in Genesis VI. There is no religion, no ancient body of myth, no archaic legacy of belief or ritual, which does not exhibit some record, some allusion to the descent on earth of creatures more perfect than the human species.

Once again, of course, a totally spurious parallelism is being invoked. That we are now in the process of revising our whole estimate of the observational skills of prehistoric communities; that it looks as if megalithic stone circles and alignments, from the Balearic islands to the Hebrides, may have been rather precise astronomical and seasonal pointers; that our notion of linear evolution is being challenged in some measure by a subtler, more cyclical model—these are genuine facts, susceptible of rational investigation, susceptible of criticism and of refutation. They have nothing to do with the portentous imbecilities of the UFO craze or with the fantasy of galactic embassies. Yet both these topics have spawned a publishing vogue, indeed a publishing industry, which runs into millions of copies of magazines, pamphlets, and books.

The term astral relates to a second great class of mumbo-jumbo. The occult is now a vast industry with multifarious sub-divisions. Psychic, psychokinetic, telepathic phenomena are being studied with the utmost seriousness. Clairvoyants of every hue flourish, ranging from the lady of the tea leaves on the amusement pier, to practitioners of graphology, palmistry, geomancy, and the Tarot pack. If ectoplasm is just now a little out of favour, having led to the detection of primitive fraud in every case fairly examined, media are not. It is simply that the old table-rapping routine and the veiled lamp have yielded to more suave techniques of magnetic aura and hypnosis. Extra-sensory perception is formidably in vogue. Basing itself on such occurrences as déjà-vu; deriving crude analogies from the existence of electromagnetic fields around material objects and events; drawing, in a profoundly naïve way, on hypotheses of indeterminacy and complementarity in particle physics, the ESP lobby prospers.

An entire edifice of pseudo-science has been erected on the foundation of certain unquestionably interesting anomalies in human perception and in the laws of statistics, which are not, of course, laws in any irrevocable, transcendentally deterministic sense. Coincidences, many of them grossly unverifiable, are assigned uncanny weight. Kinks, or apparently anomalous clusters in what should be purely random series of happenings—the right card turning up, a better-than-average divination of concealed symbols—these are cited in evidence of an occult, animist view of the universe. Unbeknown to himself, but in ways wholly familiar to adepts of Rosicrucianism, of the Golden Lotus, of the Hidden Atlantis, modern man is enmeshed in a network of psychic forces. There are reversals or synchronisms of time in which past, present, and future overlap. The astral presences will be made manifest; the die will turn up all sixes; the number on your dog licence is the cube thrice halved of the telephone number of the beloved. The builders of the Pyramids knew, Nostradamus knew, Mme Blavatsky whispered the secret to Willie Yeats. Send for the free introductory booklet.

Again, there is a contrasting, rational analogy. But the point has to be put with extreme care.

Granted numerous sophistications, it is none the less true that our daily language and routine imaginings do still operate with a rough and ready mind-body dualism. In our unexamined recourse to such polarities as psychic and physical, mental and bodily, innate and environmental, we have scarcely improved very much on the dissociative schemes of Cartesian and idealist philosophy. There is, to borrow a famous idiom, a ghost in the machine and somehow the two synchronize. When we bother to reflect, to consider the evidence, we know, of course, that this crude dualism won't do. The categories are hopelessly indiscriminate; the intermediate zones, the modes of interaction and reciprocal determination, are far too manifold. Powers of suggestion do act on pain; sympathetic and hypnotic practices are often followed by the disappearance of warts; acupuncture is not a confidence trick (unless we take confidence to signify the nervous system's active acquiescence in an analgesic process). These are banal examples chosen from a wide compass of psychosomatic realities. Recent studies of the generation of human speech indicate that there is a crucial mediation between the neurophysiological or even the neurochemical matrix on the one hand, and factors which can only be termed psychic-cultural on the other. Wherever we turn—to theories of human perception, to the study of stress and psychopathology, to linguistics, to molecular biology—we do find correlative revaluations of the whole model of how the mind and body may fit together. It is by now, surely, an honest commonplace to say that consciousness acts on the environment, that consciousness is, in some sense, the environmental structure, and that the reciprocities between the immaterial and the material are ones of dynamic feedback. Everywhere, the old divorcement of spirit from flesh is yielding to a much more complex metaphor of continuum.

Similarly, there is a fundamental review in progress of such basic notions as chance, probability, law. The development of quantum physics has brought with it a philosophic debate of great intensity and great implication about the very basis of what we call objectivity. What characterizes current hypotheses on energy, on space, on the directionality of time, is an unprecedented delicacy, provisionality; even, I would say, poetic licence. The attack of the occultists and vitalists on the mechanistic determinism of the natural sciences is an attack on a straw man. The mechanism of Laplace, or of the nineteenth-century thermo-dynamicists, if such it was, has been largely undermined, not by mystery-mongers, but by the exact and mathematical sciences themselves. Very recent conjectures in cosmology even allow the possibility that physical constants and the laws of mass-energy relation have altered in the history of the universe. The present state of the arts is one of unparalleled speculative largesse.

Compared to such considerations, the claims of the new magi, of the clairvoyants, of the spoon benders, are utterly boring and mechanical. This is the crucial issue. The advances of mathematic thought, the advances of empirical science into the as yet unknown, provide theoretic answers each of which, in turn, poses questions at an even higher level of complexity, at an even higher level of conceptual wealth and wit. The images of the world, of the place of consciousness in reality, which emerge from science, beggar our expectations and means of expression. By contrast, the explanations put forward by believers in astral emanations, in cosmic collisions, in occult forces from the fifth dimension, are utterly predictable and reactionary. They juggle counters and fantasms as old as human fear itself. They would impose on the measureless complexity and wit of the facts, as we learn to decipher them, a crude regimentation. Anti-matter and neutron stars are working conjectures as deep, as elegant, as great music; little green men with pointed ears or the ventriloquist's forgery of the voices of our dear departed are simply a bore. Or to put it another way, there is undoubtedly much more in heaven and earth than was dreamt of in Horatio's philosophy. But who ever affirmed that Horatio was a great philosopher?

There is, moreover, a nastier side to the ouija-board. *The Exorcist* is only the most calculated, nauseating, amongst innumerable exploitations of the vogue for the occult. Satanic trash is now pouring out of books, magazines, films, seances, or the homicidal pornography which follows on such events as the Manson murders. The assertion that malign agencies are abroad and must be assuaged, is a deliberate exploitation of human fears and miseries. Remember that in magic there is always blackmail.

The third of the major spheres of unreason is that which could be entitled Orientalism. It is by no means new. The recourse to wisdom from the East is habitual to Western feeling from the time of the Greek mystery cults to Freemasonry and beyond. It registers a dramatic upswing during the 1890s. It inspires the work of Hermann Hesse, of C. G. Jung and, to some extent at least, of T. S. Eliot. Since the Second World War, it has turned to a veritable flood.

The flower children wend their way to Katmandu. The scalped, saffron-robed votaries of Hare Krishna bounce down Broadway and Piccadilly jingling their tambourines. The matron and the entrepreneur contemplate their deliquescent physique in the mournful stretch of the Yoga class. The joss stick burns softly under the mandala poster, the Tibetan peace sign, the prayer rug in the bed-sitter in Santa

Monica or Hammersmith. In the university of Bacon and Newton, of Darwin and of Bertrand Russell, a thousand students crowd to the Maharishi's sandalled feet. We meditate; we meditate trancendentally; we seek Nirvana in suburban trances. Teenage butter balls descend upon us via Air India, proclaim themselves to be the Way and the Light, offer ineffable clichés on the healing powers of Love, and scatter petals from their pudgy fingers. We fill the stadium to hear their revelation. It turns out that they are cunning mountebanks, and currency speculators. The Light and the Tao shine undimmed. "What is the sound of one hand clapping?" asks the Master of Zen. "The star is the Lotus; ommani padme ... ", mumble the Cook's Tour's lamas. Tanka and guru, haiku and dharma; an irridescent flim-flam has entered our speech.

It is not so much these externals that count; they may pass as did the rage for Chinoiseries in eighteenth-century cabinet making. It is the implicit idealization of values eccentric or contrary to the Western tradition. Passivity against will; a theosophy of stasis or eternal return against a theodicy of historical progress; the focused monotony, even emptiness, of meditation and of meditative trance as opposed to logical, analytic reflection; asceticism against prodigality of person and expression; contemplation versus action; a polymorphic eroticism, at once sensual and self-denying, as against the acquisitive, yet also sacrificial, sexuality of the Judaeo-Hellenic inheritance: these are the terms of the dialectic. The undergraduate fingering his prayer beads or contemplating a Zen koan as he drifts into a melancholy haze, the worn executive hurrying to his meditation class or lecture on the karma, are seeking to ingest more or less modish, pre-packaged elements of cultures, rituals, philosophic disciplines which are, in actual fact, fiercely remote, various, and difficult of access. But he is also, and this is more important, articulating a conscious or instinctual critique of his own values, of his historical identity. The trek to Benares or Darjeeling is an attempt to break out of the shadow of our own condition.

These tides of irrationalism—astrological, occult, Oriental—are obviously symptoms. What are the underlying causes? Where they engage phenomena so widespread and confused, generalizations are bound to be inadequate. But because we touch here and there on the very springs of our contemporary climate, and of our theme, in these lectures, certain guesses may be worth making.

It is a truism to say that Western culture is undergoing a dramatic crisis of confidence. Two world wars, the return to political barbarism of which the holocaust was only the most bestial example, continual inflation—a factor which corrodes the structure of society and of personality in ways at once radical and not yet fully understood—these have provoked a widespread failure of nerve. Already sapped by rationalism and the scientific-technological point of view, organized religion, and Christianity in particular, proved helpless, and indeed corrupt, in the face of the massacre of World War One, and in the face of totalitarian and genocidal terrors thereafter. It is not often said plainly enough. Those who realize that the same church blessed the killer and the victim, that the churches refused to speak out and pursued, under the worst terror ever visited upon civilized man, a policy of unctuous silence, those who know these things are not surprised by the bankruptcy of any theological stands since.

Yet the very recrudescence of these great homicidal political terrors, the reversion to techniques of falsehood, torture, and intimidation which the late eighteenth and the nineteenth centuries had confidently regarded as nightmares dissipated for good from civilized humanity, these demonstrated the inadequacy of the Enlightenment and of secular reason. Again, we should not forget that the rationalist prediction went terribly, tragically wrong also. It is not easy to think back on the conviction of Voltaire, a conviction voiced with complete confidence 300 years ago, that torture would never again become an instrument of politics among European and Western men. In other words, there has been no place to turn. At the very moment when, in the guise of concentration camps and police states, men were translating Hell from a mythical underground to a mundane reality, the promise of a compensatory Heaven—the church promise—was all but dissipated. At the same time, the liberal humanist contract had been broken. That contract underwrites Western thought from Jefferson and Voltaire to Matthew Arnold and perhaps to Woodrow Wilson. It has now been torn to bits. The impact of this dual failure on the Western psyche has obviously been destructive—I have tried to analyze this process in more detail in previous writings.

Damaged by catastrophe, living under the palpable threat of self-destruction through atomic weapons and the seemingly insoluble problems of overpopulation, famine, and political hatred, men and women began looking, literally, outside the earth. The Flying Saucer—whose appearance in the mind's eye Jung had precisely foretold—represents an infantile but perfectly understandable wish-fulfilment. Incapable of coping with his own circumstance, man hopes desperately for benevolent, all-seeing surveillance, and in the extreme case, for help from outside. The space creatures will not allow the human species to wipe itself out. Being infinitely more evolved then we are, the space creatures will bring answers to our desperate dilemmas. Humanity may well have suffered apocalyptic breakdowns before this. Somehow, we are told, the species survived and the spiral of progress began anew. Our space guardians no doubt played a salutary role in these previous cataclysms; witness the spoors of their visitations; witness man's homage to such supernatural helpers as recorded in religions, mythologies, and primitive art. Just before our lunatic politicians press the thermonuclear button, some galactic personage will step out of his UFO and look upon us with severe, but finally therapeutic, melancholy.

The Western sense of failure, of potential social-political chaos, has also caused a revulsion against the ethnic and cultural centralism which marks European and Anglo-Saxon thought from ancient Athens to the 1920s. The assumption that Western civilization is superior to all others, that Western philosophy, science, political institutions, are manifestly destined to rule and transform the globe, is no longer self-evident. Many Westerners, the young especially, find it abhorrent. Appalled by the folly of imperialist wars, outraged by the ecological devastation which Western technology has entailed, the flower child and the freak-out, the Symbionese liberationist, and the dharma bum have turned to other cultures. It is the traditions of Asia, of the American Indian, of the black African, which draw him. It is among these that he finds those qualities of dignity, communal solidarity, mythological invention, involvement in the vegetable and animal orders, which Western man has lost or brutally eradicated. In this quest for innocence there is often a legitimate impulse to reparation. Where the colonialist father has massacred and exploited, the hippie son seeks to preserve or to make good.

Yet, powerful and ubiquitous as they are, these great reflexes of fear and compensation in the damaged sensibility of the West, seem to me a secondary phenomenon. The return to the irrational is, first and foremost, an attempt to fill the emptiness created by the decay of religion. Beneath the great surge of unreason there is at work that nostalgia for the absolute, that hunger for the transcendent, which we observed in the mythologies, in the totalizing metaphors of the Marxist utopia, of man's liberation, in Freud's scheme of complete sleep of Eros and Thanatos, in Lévi-Strauss's punitive, apocalyptic science of man. The absence of a commanding theology of a systematic mystery such as was incarnate in the church, is equally graphic in the fantasies

48

of the UFO spotter, in the hopes and panics of the occultist, in the amateur adept of Zen. That the search for alternative realities through the use of psychedelic drugs, through a dropping out from consumer society, through the manipulations of trance and ecstasy, are directly related to the hunger for the absolute is obvious—though the particular dynamics of the relationship, notably in the case of narcotics, is more complex than was at first supposed. And I ask only in passing—does it have genetic correlates? Does it reflect the actual destination of the educated elite, particularly in France and England in the First World War? The sleep of reason crowds this emptiness with nightmares and illusions.

For this, I believe, is what the post-religious or surrogate theologies and all the varieties of the irrational have proved to be—illusions. The Marxist promise is cruelly bankrupt. The Freudian programme of liberation has been only very partially fulfilled. The Lévi-Straussian prognostication is one of ironic chastisement. The Zodiac, the spooks, and the platitudes of the guru will not still our hunger.

One further alternative remains. The foundation of personal existence on the pursuit of the objective scientific truth: the way of the philosophic and exact sciences. But has it a future?

In the four preceding talks, I have argued that the gradual erosion of organized religion and of systematic theology, particularly of Christian religion in the West, has left us with a deep, unsettling nostalgia for the absolute. Together we have looked briefly at some of the principal attempts to satisfy this nostalgia, to fill the vacuum of personal faith and to attempt to fill the great emptiness left by the erosion of religious practice. I have called these attempts "mythologies" in order to underline their own pseudo-religious and substitute quality. But I hope that I have also stressed their rational character, the rational splendour of such great constructs of analysis and explanation as we find in Marxism, in Freudian psychology, in the anthropology of Claude Lévi-Strauss. Whatever their metaphoric and even mystical attributes, these are monuments of reason and celebrations of the ordering powers of rational thought. In my fourth talk, I said something of the irrationalities, superstitions, infantile escapism, surrender to hocus-pocus, which are so striking, so disturbing, a feature of the current emotional climate and life-style.

In this argument, the great absence has, of course, been that of science. It was precisely the belief that the natural sciences would fill—indeed more than fill—the emptiness left in the human spirit by the decay of religion and supernaturalism, which was one of the major forces bringing about this decay. To the philosophers of the Enlightenment, to the agnostic and pragmatic thinkers of the nineteenth century, the rise of the sciences—mathematical, physical, social, applied—was causally and logically inseparable from the decline of religion. As the ancient darkness of unreason and credulity receded, the light of the sciences was to shine forth. The "impassioned countenance" of scientific discovery, to borrow Wordsworth's phrase, would replace the childish mask of the gods and serve as a beacon for human progress. Indeed, as Auguste Comte and Marx argued, religion itself would be recognized as having been little more than a pre-science, a naïve, anthropomorphic attempt by the human species to understand, to grapple with, the natural world and its many enigmas. By moving from the spurious explanations of theology and the sterile techniques of ritual to genuine scientific understanding, man would not only achieve immense material gains, he would satisfy the cravings of the human spirit and of the human soul for truth. Seen in this perspective—a perspective which extends from Jefferson and the Humboldts to Darwin and Bertrand Russell—science would, in a way far surpassing that of revealed religion, satisfy man's aspirations for order, for beauty, for moral probity. "The truth", we are told (John 8, 32), "shall make you free." But can science assuage the nostalgia, the hunger for the absolute? What, today, is the status of the classical concept of truth?

The disinterested pursuit of the truth in a sense which Descartes or Sir Karl Popper understand it—as subject to falsification, to experimental proof, to logical constraint—this pursuit is not a universal. I know this is an unfashionable thing to affirm, but the disinterested hunt for abstract truth is culturally specific; its history is relatively brief, it has a geography of its own. It is an Eastern Mediterranean phenomenon which in turn energized the Western intellectual and scientific tradition. Why did it originate where it did (in Asia-Minor, in Greece, somewhere around the end of the seventh, or perhaps the start of the sixth century

B.C.)? This is a very difficult question, possibly related to factors of climate, of protein diet, of a masculine-dominated kinship system in which men were predatory and had a dominant questing role. Perhaps there would not have been pure, speculative thought without slavery, without the fact that men had leisure, to give their will and energy and ambitions to problems not immediately related to economic and personal survival. In other words, the pursuit of truth is, from the outset, a pursuit. It has elements of the hunt and of conquest. There is a characteristic moment in one of Plato's dialogues when at the end of a very difficult, logical demonstration, the disciples and the crowds standing around, give a literal "Haloo", the cry of the hunter when he has cornered his quarry.

Through the scientific-technological revolution which came to dominate Western social and psychological consciousness after the sixteenth century, the entire conception of truth assumes both a more special rigour and an almost unexamined moral obviousness and authority. The mathematiçal, the logical, character of propositions embodying the truth greatly increases the attributes of abstraction, of neutrality, of impersonality. Men begin feeling that the truth is somewhere "out there". It's an awkward phrase, it's hard to explain, but I think we all know what we mean: as if it were out of the reach of our hand and had an existence of its own.

When Kant tries to explain how the human brain organizes perceptions of cause, of space, of time, what he is, in fact, doing is saying, look, we live in a world which Newton has explained, and we have had imprinted in the human mind, these primary categories, as he calls them. We might call them searchlight beams, ways of understanding the universe so that we somehow get it right. At the same time both the Renaissance and the Enlightenment made it an axiom, quite undebated, that human prosperity, human dignity, the moral excellence of the individual man, the splendour of society, can only benefit from the determination of the truth and from the constant discovery of new truths.

The promise which we find in the Gospel, that the truth shall make us free, became a cardinal article of secular rationalism and of political liberalism. You find it in a very moving way inscribed to this day on public libraries all over the United States. It is a crucial Jeffersonian moment of trust. Pursue the truth, get it right, and you will be a more complete, a freer human individual. The scholar, the scientist, were the benefactors of mankind whose often bizarre, seemingly private labours must be underwritten by society. The jokes about eccentric great scientists falling down a well when they are looking at stars, or Archimedes being so busy with an abstract problem in Algebra that he doesn't notice that the city has fallen and he is about to be killed, go right back to the beginning of Greek philosophy and they are deeply suggestive. They are jokes about human genius being strange and bizarre. But they never put in doubt the essential excellence of the pursuit of the disinterested fact and discovery. From the Renaissance through to the late nineteenth century, we find it an axiom that human progress is totally enmeshed with the pursuit of facts and with the application or expression of that pursuit in the arts, in the humanities, in the sciences, and in technology.

There are from the beginning, it is true, strong dissenting voices. The mystical tradition, which I might call the part of Asia inside Western man, has from the time of the Gospels on right to modern times, always insisted on a vision of truth beyond rational grasp, beyond logic, beyond experimental control or refutation. It is said, somewhere there is a "truth higher than truth", of immediate mystical revelation. The churches have fought back. They have said that the truth is in their keeping. It is revealed to man by divine intervention. The long struggle of the Catholic church, for example, against Galileo is the struggle of a revealed total image of the universe against the threat of change, against fragmentation. The Renaissance church was very shrewd in believing that the new astronomy would unsettle and hence expose to arbitrary challenge the very concept of proof and of truth. They saw that once a Galileo had been at work, an Einstein, as it were, might come and say to Galileo, you too are wrong. And it is this unpredictable instability of the searching mind which the church felt as a profound menace to human order and human happiness.

The subtlest attack on the notion of truth has actually come in modern times. It has been propounded by a group of philosophers who are usually called the Frankfurt school. They lived and worked in the German city of Frankfurt and around an institute of sociology at Frankfurt University in the years immediately preceding and following the Second World War. Some of the names we associate with this movement are those of Marcuse and Ardorno and Horkheimer. They say something profoundly unsettling. Their argument goes something like this. Objectivity, scientific law, truth-functions, indeed logic itself, are neither neutral nor eternal but express the world view, the economic power-structure, the political ideals of the ruling class, and, in particular, the bourgeoisie in the West. The concepts of an abstract truth, of an ineluctable objective fact, are themselves weapons in the class struggle. Truth, in their explanation, is in fact a complex variable dependent on political social aims. Different classes have different truths. There is no objective history, they claim, but only the history of the oppressor. There is no history of the oppressed. Logic is a weapon of the literate bureaucracy as against the intuitive sensory modes of speech and feeling among the less-well-educated masses. The enshrinement of scientific laws, whether Newtonian, Darwinian, or Malthusian, reflects a conscious investment in intellectual and technological control over society.

The anarchic pastoralism of today's counter-culture

movements, which we touched on in the fourth talk—the visionary abdication of the drop-out, the utopias of the alternative technology, the revolt against science—so prominent among many of our gifted young contemporaries, all these embody strong elements of these three lines of attack—mystical, religious, political–dialectical. They remind us of Blake's anti-rationalism, of his repudiation of sequential discourse and logic in the name of egalitarian and anarchic commitments. They tell of his famous attack on Newton as having somehow split and rendered dry and inhuman the magic of the rainbow. Today these forces against the truth which were once scattered and diverse, are powerfully joined in a general, political, moral attitude.

But there is also, and I think far more worryingly, for the first time in the Western tradition, an incongruence, a coming out of phase, between truth and human survival, between the rational pursuit of truth and contrasting ideals of social justice. It is not only that the truth may not make us free, but that it may destroy us.

Let me give three examples in an ascending order of immediacy of risk. And the first one, I immediately admit, is deliberately remote. In a great leap of human imagination, as great as any accomplished by poets, artists, musicians, philosophers, a group of thermodynamic thinkers between the late 1840s and 1860s worked out what we know as the second principle of thermodynamics—the principle of entropy, of the run-down of the universe. Let me quote from Bertrand Russell:

> The second law of thermodynamics makes it scarcely possible to doubt that the universe is running down, and that ultimately nothing of the slightest interest will be possible anywhere. Of course, it is open to us to say that when the time comes God will wind up the machinery again: but if we do say this, we can base our assertion only upon faith, not upon one shred of scientific evidence. So far as scientific evidence goes, the universe has crawled by slow stages to a somewhat pitiful result on this earth and is going to crawl by still more pitiful stages to the condition of universal death.

Now you may rightly say, look, don't worry about things billions and billions of years hence which we cannot even imagine. I agree with you. But I'm not quite sure that the argument is that simple. What fascinates me is how near does a date have to come in order to begin worrying us? The decay of the solar system, the problem of the decay of our galaxy: At which point would the human imagination suddenly have that most terrifying insight that the future tense runs into a wall, that there is a reality to which the future tense of our verb "to be" cannot apply, in which it will have no meaning whatever? When will these walls of entropy, of the heat-death of the universe, as it is called, press in our sense of an eternal possibility of life?

The second example comes much nearer home and is obviously more realistic. Evidence is accumulating that it is very hard for man, particularly for so-called developed, highly skilled and technologically equipped man to endure long periods of peace. There is considerable disagreement on the nature of the pressures which build up inside us. One image I have heard used—and it is suggestive—is a quite simple one. When you do not exercise a muscle, a strongly trained muscle, for a certain length of time, acids, a kind of poisonous toxicity, actually accumulate in the fibres. Everything begins to ache, to decay, to torment the body. One has to get moving, one has to use it again.

It does look as if great forces of ennui, of boredom, build up inside complex social systems and strain for a violent release. In that case war would not be a kind of hideous stupidity of the politicians, an accident, which the sane mind could surely have avoided. No, it would be a kind of essential balancing mechanism to keep us in a state of dynamic health. And even as we say this we know that it's an horrendous absurdity, because we are now at a point where, if we pursue this line of thought, we come up against wars from which there is no survival, no second chance, no repair of the equilibrium of the body politic.

My third example of the kind of truth which is dangerous to the survival of society is yet more present, yet more immediate. Here I have to proceed with very great care, if only because I have no professional competence whatever. You and I are rather bewildered by the charges and counter-charges flying in the camp of genetics—the whole argument about race and intelligence. There are those who tell us that some races are destined never to achieve a certain level of the intelligence quotient, or a certain level of intellectual performance, whereas other races have, as it were, an inborn advantage in the many departments of intellectual achievement which today determine the power structure of the world. Other scientists say, do not listen to that rubbish. I.Q. is a Western-organized test, it is itself a piece of blackmail against other kinds of cultures and skills—these are Nazi theories parading under pseudo-scientific respectability. The argument gets more and more bitter. And it is extremely hard for the layman to arrive at any clear picture of what is being said and what kind of evidence is being offered. So let me put a hypothetical point—and may I beg you to underline the word "hypothetical" with three red pencils at least. *Suppose* it emerges that the guess of a number of scientists is right: that environment, however excellent, however carefully handled, accounts for something like 20% or less of a human being's endowment and future chances, and that 80% or more of what you and I *are* is programmed genetically and by racial inheritance. *Suppose* this were true—what do we do with that kind of knowledge? Because all sorts of political and social consequences could follow at once—in terms of education, of access to political power, to economic skills—do we close the door? Do we say, all right, we are not interested in your results, we do not even want to know them. Society has not reached a point of wisdom, of sanity and balance, in which it can handle that kind of dynamite. Stop your research. We won't finance it. We won't accredit your laboratories. We won't give degrees for theses written in that field. (These are not journalistic suggestions. They are being put forward now by very serious, humane, and profoundly worried scientists, sociologists, and academics.) Or do we say, on the contrary, all right, go ahead, pursue your research to whatever end of truth it leads to. And if the end is totally unbearable in moral terms, in terms of human hopes, of equity, of social coherence, the devil with it— that's how the universe is built, and we simply cannot stop researching. I repeat, this is not a fantasy problem. It is upon us right now. And it is only one of a number of dramatic instances in which the ancient tradition of going after the facts at any price is beginning to come up against walls of absolute social danger and even impossibility.

The critiques of truth which I referred to earlier, the anguish being caused by these kinds of debates, have today caused a very powerful nostalgia for innocence in the politics of the young. We are told on every hand that we ought to abandon 'pure research', that we should dismantle what is called the academic prison house, that we can put the Cartesian brain to pasture while instinct plays. We are told by scientists now very much in vogue that our Western affliction with the truth is indeed an affliction. As I understand the theory, it has something to do with the fact that we have mainly used the left half of our brain, the verbal, the Greek half, the ambitious, the dominating, the mastering half. In that neglected right half lies love, intuition, mercy, the more ancient, organic ways of experiencing the world and not taking it by the throat. We are urged to give up the proud image of homo sapiens—man the knower, man the hunter after knowledge—and to go over to that enchanting vision—homo ludens, which means, quite simply, man, the player of games, man the relaxed, the intuitive, the pastoral being. Not the research for the illusory, for the possibly destructive fact, but the quest for self, for identity, for community—these, we are urged, matter supremely if we are not to commit literal social suicide. Perhaps—and this is being said by men of great integrity—perhaps there can be low-energy alternative technologies, recyling, conservation, a kind of attempt to undo those rapacities, those suicidal savageries of the industrial revolution, to which we referred in relation to Lévi-Strauss. If there can be what is called an alternative technology, why not an alternative logic, an alternative mode of thought and feeling? Before he was a hunter and killer, man was a gatherer of berries just on the edge of the Garden of Eden.

To this I would very tentatively give the following answers. I do not think it will work. On the most brutal, empirical level, we have no example in history (short of the massive military or wartime destruction) of a complex economic and technological system backtracking to a more simple, primitive level of survival. Yes, it can be done individually. We all, I think, in the universities now have a former colleague or student somewhere planting his own organic food, living in a cabin in the forest, trying to educate his family far from school. Individually it might just work. Socially, I think, it is moonshine.

Secondly, and more important, it goes against the history of our cortex, of the brain as we in the West have used it. In our cortex, the pursuit of truth is, I believe, fatally imprinted—and I know that when I'm using the word imprint, I am borrowing a problematic metaphor. Imprinted, I think, through diet, climate, economic margins, which first triggered the innate potentiality of those miraculous and dangerous human beings, the ancient Greeks, into a great and continuous explosion of genius.

If I am at all right, we are going to continue to ask questions over and over again. The German philosopher, Heidegger, puts it well. He says, questions are the piety, the prayer, of human thought. I am trying to put it a little more brutally. We, in the West, are an animal built to ask questions and to try and get answers regardless of the cost.

59

We will not institutionalize human innocence. We may try, locally, here or there. We may try to deal more carefully with the environment. We may try to avoid some of the brutal wastage, some of the truly inane inhumanities and cruelties towards animals, towards less privileged human beings, which mark even the great years of the Renaissance and the Enlightenment. This surely must be.

But at the really important end of the stick, we are a fairly cruel carnivore built to move forward, and built to move over and against obstacles. In fact, the obstacle magnetically draws us. There is something central in us which prefers difficulty, which goes for the tangled question. At the higher end, this is because the most gifted, the most energetic, among us have long known— without perhaps articulating this knowledge—that the truth is more complex than man's needs, that it may in fact be wholly extraneous and even inimical to these needs. Let me try and explain that.

It was a deeply optimistic belief, held by classical Greek thought and certainly by rationalism in Europe, that the truth was somehow a friend to man, that whatever you discovered would finally benefit the species. It might take a very long time. Much of research clearly had nothing to do with immediate economic or social benefits. But wait long enough, think hard enough, be disinterested enough in your pursuit, and between you and the truth which you had discovered there will be a profound harmony. I wonder whether this is so, or whether this was itself our greatest romantic illusion? I have a kind of picture of the truth waiting in ambush round a corner for man to come near— and then getting ready to club him on the head. In the three examples I've given—and there are many more—we may get a rather terrifying picture of a universe which was in no way built for our comfort, for our survival, let alone for our economic and social progress on this tiny Earth.

We are told today by the champions of ecology that we are guests on this Earth. This is undoubtedly the case. And we are surely guests in a very vast and incomprehensibly powerful universe whose facts, whose relations, were not tailored to our size or our needs. Yet it is the eminent dignity of our species to go after truth disinterestedly. And there is no disinterestedness greater than that which risks and perhaps sacrifices human survival.

The truth, I believe, does have a future; whether man does is much less clear. But I cannot help having a hunch as to which of the two is the more important.